MASERATI
HERITAGE

MASERATI HERITAGE

David Sparrow and Iain Ayre

First published in Great Britain in 1995
by Osprey, an imprint of Reed Consumer
Books Limited, Michelin House,
81 Fulham Road, London SW3 6RB and
Auckland, Melbourne, Singapore and Toronto.

ISBN 1 855 324 415

Editor Simon McAuslane
Project Editor Shaun Barrington
Page design Paul Kime/Ward Peacock
Partnership

Printed in Hong Kong

Half title page
*The Bologna trident is a trademark that
has been seen on generations of
Maseratis*

Title page
*The Ghibli shows the state of play at
Maserati in the early Nineties: the
Biturbo generation has evolved into cars
with a faster and more aggressive
attitude*

Right
*The Kyalami, like many middle period
Maseratis, took its name from a wind.
Very few of them were used as vans,
even by art galleries*

For a catalogue of all books published by Osprey Automotive
please write to:

**The Marketing Department, Reed Consumer Books,
1st Floor, Michelin House, 81 Fulham Road, London SW3 6RB**

Contents

Six cylinders mean two three-into-one exhaust pipes curling away towards the shapely tail of a 250F Grand Prix racer

Officina Alfieri Maserati SpA

In the middle of the last century the industrial revolution was in full swing, and it moved on railway tracks. Throughout Europe, the railway engineers were at the sharp end, pushing at the barriers of technology in much the same way as information technology is being pushed today.

One such railway engineer lived in Voghera, near Milano. His name was Maserati and he had six sons: one, Marco, became a painter, and the others, Alfieri, Bindi, Carlo, Ernesto and Ettore became engineers. Carlo and Ernesto raced motorcycles around the turn of the century, and raced cars as well whenever they got the chance. Alfieri was a test driver for Isotta-Fraschini, and from time to time he was also employed to race their cars. Alfieri's brothers Bindi and Ettore worked at the Isotta-Fraschini factory as well.

In 1914, Alfieri changed direction: he was still heavily involved with the racing side of Isotta-Fraschini, but the relationship was on more of a freelance basis, and he founded the Oficina Alfieri Maserati SpA in December of 1914. As well as continuing to work closely with Isotta-Fraschini on developing their racing programme, serving really as a small semi-independent tuning shop, the little company was making spark plugs, the first automotive items actually to bear the name Maserati.

In 1919, brother Ernesto joined the company, and the first Maserati car was built. This, as one might have expected, was largely constructed from Isotta-Fraschini parts, and was in fact a shortened racing Isotta-Fraschini chassis originally intended to be powered by a conventional four-cylinder engine. Into this chassis was fitted an Isotta engine constructed from one bank of a V8 originally intended for aviation use. As you can imagine, the result was light and powerful, and proved to be quite rapid.

The tie with Isotta-Fraschini's racing was overshadowed by the new involvement with the Diatto organisation as the twenties began. The

Whether early racing cars loosely disguised as road cars, middle period coachbuilt models or later Maserati-bodied cars, there has never been a lack of style in the Maserati brothers' creations

Maserati brothers were soon developing and racing Diatto cars with some success, and in 1924 the Diatto company commissioned a supercharged double overhead camshaft 2-litre straight eight engine in a Grand Prix racing chassis. In 1925 this hit the track for the first and, as it transpired, last time. Whether it would have developed into anything important became academic, as Diatto went bust in 1927.

For one reason or another, the straight eight Grand Prix car remained with the Maserati brothers, and they carried on working to develop it. To qualify for the 1.5-litre class, they reduced the capacity of the engine to 1500cc and relaunched it as the Maserati Tipo 26. It had been pretty well the Maserati brothers' baby from day one anyway, so it was certainly justifiable to call it a Maserati. The blown straight eight was the first car to feature the three-pronged trident symbol seen on Maseratis ever since. The car did well on its first time out in 1927, winning its class and coming ninth overall. The following year it won.

The original car was developed into a 2-litre version in the form of the 26B, and in 1929 the Maserati brothers built a monster for Formula Libre racing. Known as the Sedici Cilindri, the car featured basically two straight eight engines sharing the same crankcase and set in a V. In a straight line the car was capable of speeds in excess of 150mph, although its performance was less impressive when anything other than a straight line was involved.

Throughout the Thirties, Maserati continued making spark plugs and hand-built sports and racing cars. They were unable to achieve consistent success on the track, however. To some extent this was because they were unable to generate the necessary investment capital to stay seriously competitive and to protect their place in the front rank: this is a problem for small racing car manufacturers that has existed for very nearly a hundred years. From the racing cars, a limited number of road cars were built, fitted with coachbuilt bodies. The 4CS-1100 and the 4CS-1500 were available in 1932 and 1933. In 1938, the 8C-500 was available with a rather pretty body by Castagna.

In March of 1932, Alfieri died, as a result of an operation on old injuries sustained in a racing accident some years previously. Ettore, Bindo and Ernesto carried on to produce the three litre 8CM Grand Prix car. Financially, things continued to be relatively hard going, so the arrival on the scene of Commendatore Adolfo Orsi in 1937 was very welcome. Orsi ran an industrial combine that was involved in making machine tools and bus and railway systems, although the connection with Maserati may

There was a gradual encroachment of luxury into Maserati's interiors, but for a long time they were as basic as the interiors of the racing cars to which they were very close relations indeed

Above
The remaining Maserati brothers went off on their own to form OSCA and carry on building handmade cars, but the Maserati name stayed with the original company

Left
No compromise: open the lid on any Maserati engine bay, and there are no fripperies in sight, just large numbers of camshafts and carburettors

well have come about because the Orsi organisation made spark plugs – as did Maserati themselves.

The Maserati brothers were bought out and signed up for a ten year consultancy deal, relieving them of direct money problems, thus enabling them to concentrate on making racing cars and the occasional spin-off road car. During this period, the A6GCS car was conceived and constructed, and the 2-litre Formula 2 car was designed and built, and that in turn developed and evolved into the legendary 250F.

With Juan Manuel Fangio in the driving seat, this beautiful and seriously quick Maserati won the World Championship in 1957: one of the high points for the Maserati company. As well as the racing cars, chassis were being shipped off to various coachbuilders for a variety of bodywork to be fitted: Pinin Farina, Vignale and Frua all made their own contribution with an assortment of sports and sports racing bodies.

When their ten year consultancy contract expired, the remaining

Maserati brothers couldn't resist the pull of freedom and independence, and went off on their own to form OSCA – Officine Specializzata Costruizone Automobili. The Maserati name stayed with the Orsi family.

The 1600 Osca was a neat and attractive little car, resembling its bigger Maserati brothers in the elegance of its proportions on rather a smaller scale, and powered by a double overhead camshaft four-cylinder engine, with two huge Webers squeezed into the diminutive engine bay. The interior was typically Italian of the period: two big dials for speed and revs, a thin woodrim wheel and sparse interior comforts: after all, it was for going quickly rather than being cosseted in Grand Tourer style.

Badgework on the car was limited to OSCA 1600 on the bootlid, Fissore Savigliano on the front wings and a round badge on the front bearing the O.S.C.A. legend and a coat of arms, with 'Fratelli Maserati Bologna' running around the outside indicating that, although it wasn't a Maserati as such, it had certainly been built by the Maserati brothers.

The Maserati name and the company's racing ambitions were now firmly with the Orsi family, but even the Orsi coffers, deep though they might be, were not bottomless. When the entire works team of four Maserati 450S racing cars was written off in the same race in Venezuela in 1957, there was a considerable rethink. With the Orsi organisation in financial trouble from other directions as well, 1958 saw an air of pragmatism in the company and an increasing interest in road cars: the 3.5-litre six-cylinder engine was fitted in a tube frame intended very much for the road rather than the track. They were still very fast cars and they might still be written off once in a while, but at least the car would belong to someone else when it happened, and they could always sell him a replacement.

The 3500GT occupied Maserati from 1959 until 1964, with 2,000 of them built. The occasional foray into racing kept a little excitement in the game, and the V8 powered 5000GT with a top speed of 160 mph kept up Maserati's reputation for making seriously fast cars, although only 36 were built.

Throughout the Seventies, Maserati concentrated on low volume, expensive exotics such as the Indy, the Ghibli and the Bora. However, the rest of the world was now out of step with them, and was concerned with fuel shortages and recessions.

Most people were more concerned with keeping their Ford Anglias on the road rather than aspiring to multi-cylindered Italian exotics, and Maserati found themselves heading for the rocks. A mixed blessing was provided by the arrival of Citroën on the scene. Citroën initially bought part of the Maserati company, then came back for what was left a year or so later.

At that time, Citroën was still a maker of advanced cars, both in terms of styling and engineering, and Maseratis changed in small ways, particularly in the control systems and in the hydraulics. The most memorable result of the Citroën-Maserati connection was the SM, a radical Citroën-bodied sports GT with a Maserati engine. However, the general public admired its looks, but failed to form a significant queue to buy it.

Citroën put the Maserati company into liquidation in May of 1975, the same year that Ernesto Maserati died. Things looked bleak, but Alejandro de Tomaso put together a financial package with Gestione e Participazione Industriali SpA, a government sponsored organisation, and bought the company out of liquidation with the aid of partners. Maserati got going again, back to building their own cars as an independent. Omer Orsi, the son of Adolfo Orsi, had provided a historical thread of continuity during this turbulent period, and remained as commercial director throughout until he retired in 1977.

The late Seventies saw a series of big and beautiful cars, design classics of their time – the Bora, Merak and Khamsin carried the Maserati name forward, although the cost and impracticality of these supercars restricted them to a small and affluent audience. 1982 saw a change of direction, in the form of a very successful move into a more mainstream market with the introduction of the Biturbo series of cars. Rather than mid-engined exotics, these were small, understated saloon cars, powered by a 2-litre engine with two turbochargers and a resultant output of 180bhp. Not up there with the 5-litre big boys, but nonetheless capable of a respectable performance, and very justifiable for a successful businessman as a practical car.

Also in the early Eighties came a tie-in with Chrysler, which had bought 5% of the De Tomaso corporation. The plan was that Maserati should develop a Chrysler-Maserati sports car, to be powered by a Lotus-derived engine. This was the brainchild of Lee Iacocca, who had been largely responsible for putting big Ford V8 engines into the De Tomaso Pantera in the Seventies. However, the project failed to realise its potential.

As time has gone by, Maserati have relied on the Biturbo idea to serve as a basis for a small but increasing range of seriously high performance derivations such as the Shamal and the recent new Ghibli: they are again expanding into the market for slightly larger luxury cars with the second generation of four-door Quattroporte cars.

The Racing Heritage

The first ever racing Maserati was the Type 26. Built in 1926, it was one of those rare blends of function and form in which the proportions are naturally correct: in short, it was a little beauty.

Developed from the earlier Diatto design, the supercharged straight eight engine was reduced in size to 1500cc. Bore and stroke were 60mm and 66mm respectively, and the bhp figure was 115 at 5,300rpm. Ready to race, its weight was 720 kilos, and the top speed hovered around the 100mph mark. Its debut was in the Targa Floria of the same year, bearing the number 5 on the scuttle. With Alfieri Maserati at the wheel, it came first in the 1.5-litre class and ninth overall.

Neptune's three-pronged trident appeared for the first time on a Maserati; it was also the symbol of the city of Bologna. In 1927, the trident symbol on the mesh grille of a Type 26 was the first thing to hurtle past the chequered flag when Alfieri won the Italian championship in 1927.

The Maserati brothers had obviously got the hang of it by now, and the racing career of the company went onward and upward with the Type 26B. This was largely the same as the Type 26, but the engine was enlarged to two litres, taking the power up to 150bhp by extending the bore and stroke to 62mm and 82mm respectively. The Type 26B was current through 1928 and 1929, and although less than a dozen were built, a few Type 26 cars were fitted with the larger engine: it is unlikely that the thought of keeping them original for posterity even crossed anyone's mind.

Predating Carroll Shelby's gung-ho approach to racing car engineering by a couple of decades, the Maserati brothers applied the 'too much is just right' rule to their next car, which was a 4-litre monster, the engine of which was constructed by amalgamating two of the straight eight racing engines on a common crankshaft. Naturally, this also involved two superchargers as well. The power output was 305bhp, and top speed was 153mph. The car had rather an evil reputation, and although extremely effective in a straight line, was something of a handful should one encounter a corner.

Above right
The glorious 250F was thought by many people to be the most beautiful GP car ever built. It was undeniably very pretty, as well as fast

Right
The cockpit of the 250F: it feels as though you are sitting on the car rather than in it, and your elbows are supposed to go outside the cockpit sides

The Type V4 achieved the fastest speed ever for a racing car at Cremona in 1929 over a 10 km circuit, and in the same year Alfieri set a lap record at Monza which stood until 1954. Considering that current lap speed records frequently only last for a matter of weeks, to hold the record for twenty-five years takes some doing: if the V4 could have been persuaded to co-operate when a corner loomed into sight, it could have been one of the all time greats rather than merely a fascinating footnote.

The 8C-1100 and 8C-1500 were developed and refined versions of the Type 26 design, with liners fitted to the cylinders to reduce the capacity of the engine, which still remained a supercharged straight eight. When the engine was enlarged again to 2500cc in the 8C-2500, the Maserati works team began to see some serious success. At Monza in 1930, Maseratis came in first, second and third places.

The next generation of Maserati Grand Prix cars was the 8CM, with three litres and a 150mph top speed. The early versions were very light and fast, but needed some chassis mods before the best handling could derived from them. However, once sorted out they were very quick: Nuvolari drove one to victory in the Belgian Grand Prix of 1933.

Maserati then developed a series of small cars with four-cylinder engines, which were originally for voiturette racing but came to be developed in other directions as well. Another double-engined monster, the V5, was built. Although very fast, it was as dangerous as the first and was abandoned after its second crash.

The first racing Maseratis that would be recognised by most motoring enthusiasts would be the style typified by the 6CM-1500 of 1936, a very popular and successful car with many wins to its credit. Although there were ups and downs for Maserati, they continued to produce a string of very good cars. A change of approach was signalled by the 4CLT series cars: the T stood for Tubular chassis, which meant lighter and stiffer cars that kept Maserati at the front of the pack.

As time went on, the Maserati GP cars became lower, wider and more streamlined: the evolution of the archetypal front engine Grand Prix car for many people came to a peak in the beautiful and very effective Maserati 250F. Prototyped in 1953, the 250F at that time ran a 2493cc straight six with 270bhp and a top speed of around 180mph. The gearbox was rear-mounted in a transaxle unit behind the seat: it was a four-speed unit at first, and later improvements included a fifth gear. The later cars also benefited from a redesigned and considerably lighter chassis. In 1957, Fangio convincingly won the Monaco Grand Prix in a lightweight 250F as a contribution to winning the World Championship in that year: the nose had got longer and an awkward bump had appeared on the bonnet, but the 250F was still a beauty.

Some of the pre-war feel of the cars was still retained; not many

The fuel cap and oil filler of the 250F: the riveted structure of the bodywork can be clearly seen in this shot of its tail

people have been privileged to drive one, but I have sat in one. You sit very much *on* the 250F rather than *in* it, with a big spindly steering wheel and a vast bonnet stretching away into the distance, and lots of elbow room for working away at the wheel. It must have felt very vulnerable indeed compared to a modern racing car with a composite monocoque, a five-point harness, shoulder high cockpit sides and a fitted seat. In a 250F, the only concession to safety is a helmet.

There was a V12 version of the 250F, which had giveaway scoops on the bonnet and fat megaphone exhausts poking out of each side of the bodywork.

The 450S represented one of the many parallel courses steered by Maserati during the late Fifties: it was a full-bodied open racing car, with a swoopy, elegant body and a 90° four-and-a-half litre V8 kicking out a

The view from the office of a Birdcage. Not a notably luxurious environment, but there has never been a shortage of people keen to clamber in

massive 400bhp. It was extremely quick, but the chassis and the brakes were never quite up to the standard demanded by the engine, although the chassis looked as though it should have been pretty effective, being a large bore tubular affair, with the central area built on two levels. However, its only notable successes were the 1957 Sebring 12 hour and the Swedish Grand Prix.

The Type 61 Birdcage Maserati is a name that even non-racing and non-Maserati enthusiasts must have heard of. It was an early example of applied spaceframe ideas, and the chassis was an intricate tracery of thin tubes, with almost every rectangle created, then braced, by a crosstube. The tracery of chassis tubes can be seen through the windscreen where the body doesn't cover it up completely. Coincidentally, the chassis also allowed a very low central body with high wings, and the result was another typically Maserati-looking car, with delicacy and grace in its lines belying, and at the same time hinting at, its potentially evil performance. The Birdcage was very light at only 600 kilos, which was the entire

Left

A 250F doing what it's best at. These historic racers are hugely valuable, but are still given surprisingly serious stick on the track

Above

The racetrack also sees later Maseratis from time to time, as the Owners' Club assemble for track days

purpose of the chassis design, and with a three-litre/four-cylinder engine giving some 250 bhp, the car became a very popular racer. Even now, Birdcage Maseratis can still be seen making lots of other contemporary historics look as though they're standing still.

As technology progressed, it began to take more and more heavy duty effort and increasingly large finances to keep within sight of pole position on the racetrack. The same skills required to build light, fast racers could equally be applied to building light, fast and beautiful sports cars – with the crucial difference that people give you money for making them, rather than taking it away from you for the privilege of driving them in competition. Within Maserati, the drift towards road cars rather than race cars was beginning to gather pace.

In the same year that Fangio took Maserati to victory in the World Championship, the down side of Grand Prix racing was also in evidence. Orsi's parent company was having severe difficulties with Argentine debts, putting a squeeze on all operations. As a last straw, all four of the

Above
The 150S was an early full-bodied racing car, designed with lightness particularly in mind. It was effective and popular in its time

Left
Historic racing is fast and furious stuff, with no quarter given or taken with respect to the age and rarity of the cars involved

Maserati team cars were written off in a series of crashes at the Venezuelan sports car Grand Prix at Caracas: Maserati were still a small company, and the loss of four cars at once was a serious blow.

Sadly, that was to be, effectively, the end of Maserati's official involvement in Grand Prix racing. However, nobody could deny that they went out in style.

Above

An early Ghibli gets a spot of exercise during a Maserati Owners' Club test day on the racetrack. With a top speed of 168mph, this is serious fun

Right

The Ghibli's 4.7 litre V8 was a direct descendant of Maserati's pure racing engines: you only have to listen to one to know that

Above
A Merak on the track: with its engine based on the Citroën/Maserati V6 and a light body, it was a quick and competent car

Right
Seen from a more oblique angle, the Merak's flying buttresses are clear. It looks quite at ease on the track

Above
The classic Maserati straight six racing engine; 2,493c and 270bhp at 8,000rpm. Seen here sitting in the engine bay of a 250F

Right
The 250F preparing for the off. Weighing 630 kilos and putting out 270bhp through crossply tyres, it was something of a handful compared to modern GP cars

Sports Racers
and Grand Tourers

The A6G series, first driven in anger in 1947, followed the Maserati tradition of developing successful racing cars and then encouraging sports car enthusiasts to buy modified versions of them to use on the road. In the early days, this had quite frequently meant buying a full racing spec Maserati open wheeler and simply fitting a set of mudguards on it, and possibly a few lights, but little more than that.

As time went on, this exercise became a little more sophisticated. The buyers were still basically planning to take a wickedly fast virtual racing car for the sheer thrill of driving at whatever speed took their fancy on the public roads. Rather than just bunging on a few cycle mudguards, the thing to do was to have a full body fitted. That way the car looked like a sports car even if it was still a racer underneath.

The A6G-derived cars were of this breed – some of them were used purely on the track, trailered there and back and fitted, increasingly, with weird and wonderful streamlined bodywork, some with straightforward racing bodies and open wheels. The A6G series cars were two-seaters, although the open wheeled track cars had such a narrow body that this was something of a technicality. The chassis consisted of two huge drainpipe sized tubes running along the sides of the car, dipping down to the sill between the axles, and a deep and narrow central transmission tunnel, with several other big bore tubes at floor level. The rest of the chassis was mostly a tracery of lightweight tubing and bulkheads to carry the assorted bodywork options.

The engine was a 2-litre straight six, with a bore and stroke of 72mm and 81mm, and a power output of 130bhp at a maximum rpm of 5,200. This gave the car a top speed of around 114mph, although this would vary according to the body shape and the weight of the whole vehicle. There was also a twin-cam version of this engine. The kerb weight of the early open cars was a light 670 kilos, and the handling was gradually developed as the years went on.

There was a quite attractive racing narrow body fitted with flared wings blended into the sides, but by 1953 the A6GCS with its full roadster bodywork was more typical of the general direction of the A6

series cars. The 1954 Mille Miglia saw a roadster A6GCS coming a creditable third overall. As well as the road/race bodies fitted by such artists as Scaglietti, some of the more mainstream road car carrozzerias such as Pinifarina were making their own contributions to the A6 chassis. The list of those who made bodies reads like a roll of honour for the world's top designers: Pinin Farina, Vignale, Guglielmo, Frua, Zagato and Allemano all provided completely different interpretations of the theme.

Some of the chromework lathered on to the various body designs suffered from an excess of zeal, but the proportions of the chassis ensured a long bonnet and a short rear end, so even on an off-day none of the bodywork makers could mess up the basic look of the car. From the early and more upright split screen 1951 Frua car to the last of the breed, built as American influences became visible in the wraparound screen of the late-fifties Zagato bodies, the fast-changing fashions of the period are reflected far better in these cars than in the mainstream. After all, each car could be different, whereas major manufacturers could

Above
With a large wire wheel wearing a fat Pirelli Cinturato taking up most of the boot space, the Frua body was more sports than tourer

Right
Six chokes for six cylinders. The 1957 Frua Spyder also featured a twin ignition system, and the engine was made in both SOHC and DOHC forms

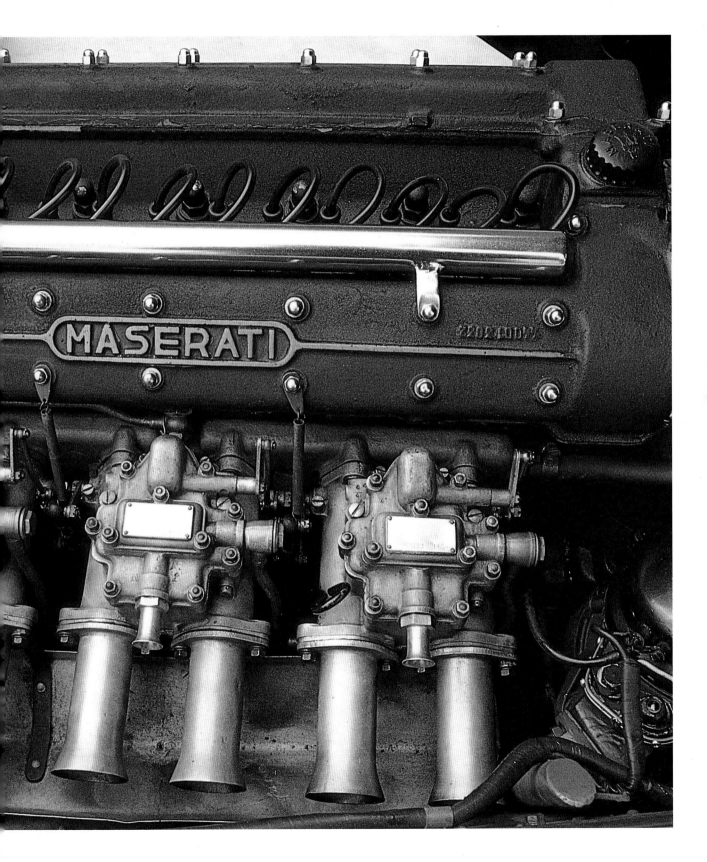

only afford a change every few years if they were particularly lucky.

The 1956 Zagato A6G 2000 coupé was one of the prettiest of the hard-top cars and, although the front looked slightly pedestrian, the general proportions and styling of the bodywork showed the best of Fifties design. Smooth, curvy and sculptured, with the length of the bonnet in perfect proportion to the rest of the body, and a low, slinky roofline dropping smoothly down to a plain, understated tail. Odd bits of chrome to break up the sides, but no bumpers at all, and the whole car squatting purposefully on spoked wheels with wide aluminium rims.

The car was no slouch either, with three Weber 38 DCO carburettors and the familiar 2-litre Maserati six. A dry weight of only 840 kilos combined with a punch of around 150bhp gave the Zagato version of the car a creditable top speed of 121mph. Quite respectable for a road car in 1956.

The 3500GT represented the change from a racing car manufacturer to a maker of cars genuinely intended for the road. 1957 saw the beginnings of the preparation of the familiar Maserati double overhead cam straight six, for pure road use. It had been on sale for what were effectively rebodied racing cars, but people who bought an A6-based car knew perfectly well that they were buying a racing car that looked like a sports car, and would accept the inherent ups and downs of racing engines on the road.

For pure road use, other criteria applied. The demands made on an engine used for commuting and shopping are generally not the same as those for racing. The 3500GT was very much a practical car, with most styles having a small back seat and a usable boot, as well as a storming performance which was there when you wanted it. The 1962 3500GT by Touring put out 235bhp, and with the weight at a substantial 1,350 kilos dry, it topped out at 146mph – very respectable by anyone's standards. The handling was also well regarded, with independent coil springs at the front and a rigid rear axle. The car still had a substantial steel chassis beneath it.

Unlike many cars with GT badges on them, this was actually a very effective Grand Tourer in all its incarnations from 1958 to 1964, in the sense that you could drive it at high speeds over long distances with people and luggage in it. Whereas, for example, the Mini 1275GT is not a Grand Tourer in any sense at all, it is merely a slightly faster Mini. When Maserati call something a GT, they mean it.

Vignale's bodies for the 3500GT were spare, elegant and modern, and

Not many convertible bodies look as good with the hood up as down, but most Frua-bodied Maseratis look just fine from any angle at all

34

the car was also improving beneath the skin. The engine was successfully being tamed into a smoother power delivery at wider rev ranges. From something of a monster, originally designed to deliver huge slugs of muscle when it was kept on the boil, either howling along the track flat-out, or crackling and backfiring as the foot came off the throttle and jammed just as hard on the brake, the engine was now required to provide turbine torque even after a thirty minute traffic jam on the Promenade des Anglais. It didn't just get smoother, however – it also got an extra 30bhp.

The Vignale-bodied cars also benefited from a slight reduction in wheelbase from 2600mm to 2500mm, which sharpened up the handling. The cars continued to go faster too, with Lucas injection an option instead of the triple Webers previously fitted. The GTI (Iniezione) badging reflected the new fuel system. Around this time, Maseratis were beginning to evolve into more recognisable and stable model types, which had been fairly difficult before; you might have bought an A6-based

Above
An aggressive look to the radiator grille: despite the stamp of the individual designer of the body, the car is still unmistakably a Maserati

Left
The dashboard looks surprisingly spartan, with much painted steel in evidence; the car is not a million miles away from its racing origins

car with a two-litre engine and a Touring body, but it was simply a Maserati rather than a Maserati Something. The 3500GT started the trend, and the Sebring was one of the first to have a name to go with its personality. 'Sebring' referred to past glory for Maserati, and the Sebring was developed from the Vignale-bodied 3500GT.

The Sebring was built in steel and was available with the 3500cc engine or options of 3700cc and 4000cc engine sizes providing yet more torque: with the introduction of front disc brakes and later all-round disc brakes, there was now more of a chance to slow down. Maserati had always been far more interested in acceleration than in retardation, but there had to be some compromises. The spirit of competition was not extinguished, however. Ferrari's Superfast engendered a typical response from Maserati in the form of the 5000GT, fitted with 450S racing engines. Some of these quadruple overhead cam V8 monsters were

The individual carrozzerias applied their own ideas to the Maserati A6G chassis, with almost universally pleasing results

Very much a shape of the period, with no shortage of chrome and detailing, and a nicely balanced coupe body

detuned for the road, but some weren't – speeds of 170mph were being bandied about for the full racing engined cars, and a detuned (310bhp) Ghia coupé was proved capable of a sustained 154mph in the hands of a German motor magazine.

The arrival of the Mistrale in 1963 signalled a change in Maserati's relationship with its coachbuilders, as the company became more involved in the car as a whole rather than simply providing a rolling chassis and leaving the carrozzerias to get on with it. The Mistrale was designed by Frua, and was a sharp and elegant design, featuring a fastback with an opening glass hatch and long, low lines that were very modern for 1963 and made the Sebring look dated. The Mistrale's body was steel, but every other panel was made in aluminium in an attempt to keep the weight down to a reasonable level. With some success, it has to be said – 1,455 kilos dry weight is not bad for a car of this size and type.

The 3,700 cc straight six produced 245bhp, giving the Mistrale a top speed of just over 150mph.

Under the crisp new body there was little change at first: the same tubular backbone chassis with outriggers, the same unequal length wishbones and coils at the front and live axle at the back on semi-elliptic springs and torque arms. Girling discs all round provided the anchors, and the engine size later went up to four litres for a little extra edge.

The Mistrale was also available in Spider form, with a claimed top speed of 159mph with the four-litre engine. While the air conditioning option underlined the new luxury grand touring aspirations of the car, failure to operate the starting procedure correctly reminded you of the car's racing origins. Full choke and one dab on the throttle and the engine would burst into life: anything other than that and it would flood, leaving you to ruminate on Maserati's racing heritage as you removed, dried and replaced twelve spark plugs before you stood any chance of firing the engine up.

Maserati's Giulio Alfieri had spent a lot of time getting the old racing V8 engine into a state where it was fit to be used in road cars, and it

Above
Again, the racing origins of the car are clearly visible in the six-cylinder engines fitted to the A6G series Maseratis

Above right
Maseratis have never been cheap: this allowed a degree of latitude to the body shops to get the details just right, irrespective of cost

Right
What were the origins of the Italians' reputation for electrical systems of doubtful efficacy, which was at its peak in the Sixties?

appeared in the first Quattroporte (or four-door) Maserati as well as in the Mexico. The Mexico was a rethink of the Quattroporte idea, designed by Vignale, who changed the car into a smaller and very competent coupé. The body was understated and a mix of modern and classical, with the V8 and the front suspension mounted in a subframe and the rest of the body constructed as a monocoque. The suspension was still traditional Maserati, with an independent coil sprung front and a rigid rear axle located via semi-elliptic springs and radius arms.

Under the subtle bodywork were giveaways as to its true nature, though: the fat Borrani-spoked wheels hinted at its potential, and the sound of the engine at full blast was something of a symphony. The buzz and chatter of four chain driven camshafts working with 32 valves, the induction roar from four huge Weber downdraughts, and the bass from eight sideplate sized pistons thundering up and down, all transmitted to the outside air via a complex twin exhaust system that wound its way around the convolutions under the car and exited under the tail via two fat chromed tailpipes.

A claimed 165 mph top speed was possibly just a little bit over-

optimistic. Nevertheless, a genuine 155mph seems to have been achievable with no bother whatsoever. Apparently, pushing one's luck in a Mexico resulted in some understeer, but this was never a major problem as it was easily corrected by the application of the right foot, which would bring the tail neatly round to balance the front. Looking at a Mexico now, it is interesting to compare the BMW CS series cars with the Mexico and to wonder which came first. The thought also occurs that not many of us will ever get our hands on a Mexico. . . but we can always buy a 635CSI and dream, can't we?

The last of the early generation of Grand Tourers emerged in 1968 in the form of the Indy. This celebrated the Maserati wins at Indianapolis in 1939 and 1940 with the Boyle Special. The car would hardly have been named after Indianapolis itself: it is a city which has been described as looking like the mouth of a very old man, a gap-toothed line of tatty old skyscrapers with spaces where tatty new skyscrapers are going up.

However, the racetrack at Indianapolis has been the scene of many a

Above
The Maserati name cast into the cam covers and a trio of Webers is a guarantee of serious and exhilarating performance

Right
The 3500GT coupe was one of the prettiest bodies of its period, with clean, balanced lines decorated with just enough chrome

historic victory, and some of these have belonged to Maserati. With the Indy, however, the reference to the racing heritage of the company was just that: Maserati certainly had a proud racing heritage, but the heritage was all that was left, as the Indy continued the move towards pure road cars rather than the Maserati's earlier tendency to sell half-detuned racing cars with bodywork superimposed on them.

The Indy was either a big front-engined GT car, with a decent amount of luggage space and a roomy 2+2 configuration, or a slightly cramped four-seat cabin, depending on your point of view, which would be largely determined by how tall you were. The engine was a 90° V8 with two camshafts for each bank of cylinders, and in its first incarnation seen at the Turin motor show of 1968, the engine size was 4200cc. At the Geneva show a year later, the engine size had been upped to 4.7 litres, in which form it put out 290bhp.

Earlier Maseratis had been built as hand-made Maserati rolling chassis to be clothed by various designers, with some delightful and graceful

Above
The test of a good car design is that it should look as good from the back as from the front: no problems here, then

Right
As the years go by, the Maserati dashboard becomes rather more upmarket, although it is still very much businesslike rather than luxurious

results. However, that was the old days, and Maserati were coming to realise that they had to concentrate much harder on the look of their bodywork if they were to get the best out of making upmarket road cars. While previously you might look at a Maserati, think it was interesting and pretty, and perhaps wonder if it was a Bertone or a Frua body, you would now look at an Indy, and think, firstly 'that's a Maserati Indy', and secondly 'I want one'.

The late sixties also saw the introduction of the Ghibli, which went head to head with the Ferrari Daytona, and in fact cost slightly more at 65,500 Swiss francs than the Ferrari's 63,000. The Ghibli was intended to change Maserati's image by being the most beautiful and overall the best two-seater Grand Tourer Maserati could come up with, and a lot of thought went into it.

The Ghibli was very long and very big at 4,590mm long and 1,800mm wide, taking up enough space for most full-sized family saloons. It is immediately plain to see, even from the most cursory glance at the gorgeous curves of the XK120 Jaguars, that a very long body is an excellent way of allowing the curves and planes of the design to develop to their greatest effect, and to get the proportions exactly the way you want them. This same rule applies to the subtle, but effective design of the Ghibli. The total lack of compromise on the looks even extended

Above
With a chassis built to the correct proportions, you can't really produce anything other than a car that looks good. Not if you're Italian, anyway

Above right
This sort of grillework is rarely seen these days: we have been conditioned to believe that painted plastic is stylish instead of merely cheap

Right
The view from the office, with the important dials right where you want them: flick your eyes down between corners to check all is well

The 3500 looks as good, or even better in Spider form. A set of Borrani wire wheels does no harm at all to the look of the car either

under the bonnet on the Ghibli, as the big V8 is quite a substantial sized lump on its own – in order to get a satisfactory low bonnet line, the engine had to be dry sumped. Even so, there's a fair sized bulge in the bonnet to accommodate the eight air intakes of the four enormous twin choke Webers controlling the breathing of the 5-litre V8.

The practical use of the car as a super luxurious Grand Tourer was not ignored either. The load space under the wide, flat rear hatch was huge enough to carry a quantity of Vuitton sufficient for even the most opulent traveller, and the air conditioning plant was designed to provide a cabin full of cool, leather-scented air a matter of some thirty seconds after it was switched on. The racing days of Maserati may have been over in practical terms, but the company was shaping up for an era of considerable success in building supercars for the road.

There is a timeless elegance to this particular body style: its lines are long enough for various subtle styling ideas to work very well

Left
The trident symbol, taken originally from the Bologna fountain, has graced the bonnets of some of the world's most attractive cars

Above
The Sebring marked a change in Maserati's approach, with much more of the car's manufacture being brought in-house

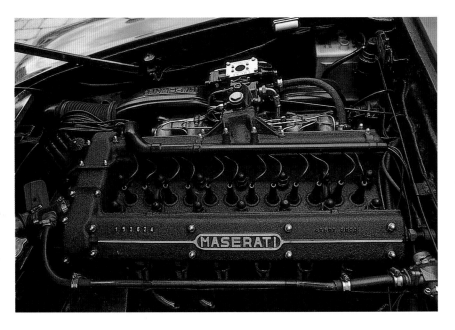

Above
By now Maserati's engines not only provided big torque and power figures: they would also tolerate traffic jams without fouling their plugs

Right
The Sebring's dash was still a matter of function rather than form, with everything of importance kept right in front of the driver

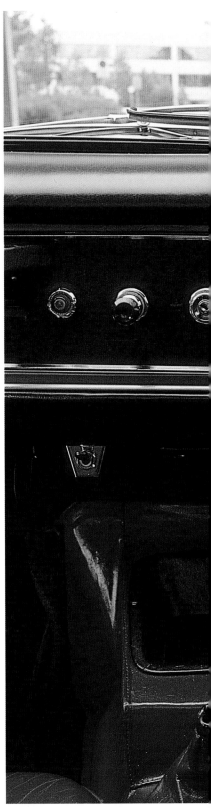

Above
The name Sebring referred to Maserati's past glories on the racetrack, although the company were now heading strongly for the GT market

Left
The Sebring's body was developed from the Vignale designed 3500GT, and was very much the product of its period

Above

The Quattroporte of the early Eighties seen from the side, showing the full size of the car: an executive express for those with subtle tastes

Left

The same Quattroporte: quietly elegant, and so understated you would hardly know it was a Maserati at all until it was started up

The Quattroporte of the Sixties was very much echoed by the later versions of the car: contemporary but understated styling, with serious performance

Above
The engine of the earlier Quattroporte combined saloon car smoothness with considerable grunt if you kept your foot down

Above right
In parallel with Ferrari, Italian dashboard design was beginning to involve separate instrument pods rather than flat dash panels

Right
Just in case you thought you were looking at an ordinary car, the Bologna trident is there to remind you that it's a Maserati

Above
… and if you still hadn't got the message, here it is in black and white — or rather in chrome plate

Above right
The towbar fitted to this Quattroporte suggests confidence in the torque figures. It is to be hoped that it was used to tow a speedboat, rather than a caravan - heaven forfend!

Right
No shortage of chrome plating anywhere on the car: American styling influences can be seen in the twin headlamp cluster and squared-off bezel

Above
Named after a wind found in southern France, the Mistrale was one of many Maseratis named after winds

Right
The Mistrale Spider was a Frua design, a relatively small Maserati with a straight six engine: wire wheels were standard

Above
Viewed from above, the pleasing proportions of the Mistrale can clearly be seen: everything is pretty well exactly in the right place

Right
Beneath the stylish bonnet of the Mistrale lurked a powerful six-cylinder engine that rose in capacity to a final size of four litres

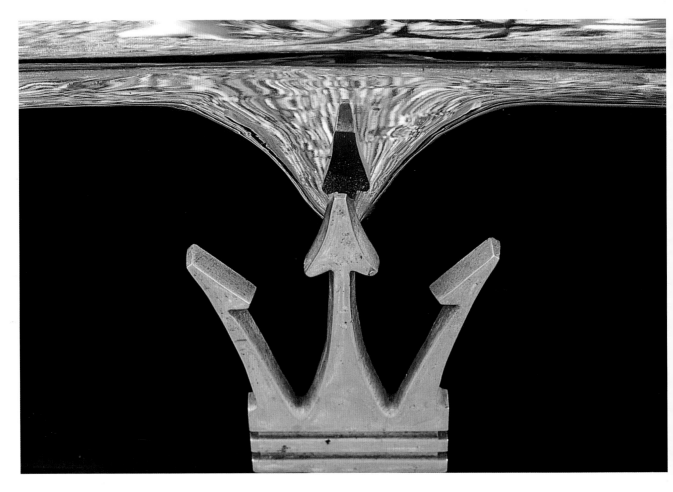

Above
If you weren't completely clear about exactly what the Mistrale was, the grille featured a crystal clear reminder of its origins and performance

Right
The power bulge and air scoops on the bonnet were as much practical as decorative: but decorative they certainly were

Above

Iniezione – Italian for Injection. Around this time the traditional triple Weber carburettors were beginning to be replaced by fuel injection systems

Right

The interior of the Mistrale was still very much a functional environment, but luxury was beginning to creep in with leather seats and thick carpets

The Mistrale in coupé form was as elegant as the open car, with a big rear window and hatch rising to reveal a useful luggage space

Above

The Mistrale coupé featured a dashboard and interior that pointed the way for future Maseratis, with increasing wood and leather in evidence

Above right

The big six-cylinder engine provided a perfect balance of usable torque and serious power for high speed cross-country driving

Right
The new injection systems being fitted to Maseratis of the period were part of the reason for the superb performance of the engines

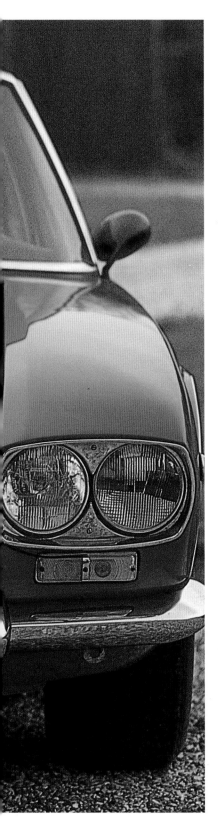

Above

The Mexico's styling was clean, sharp and well balanced, with a big glasshouse and light, delicate lines rather belying its performance

Left

The 4.7 litre Mexico was first seen at the 1966 Turin Motor Show, and featured a quad-cam V8 of nearly 300bhp

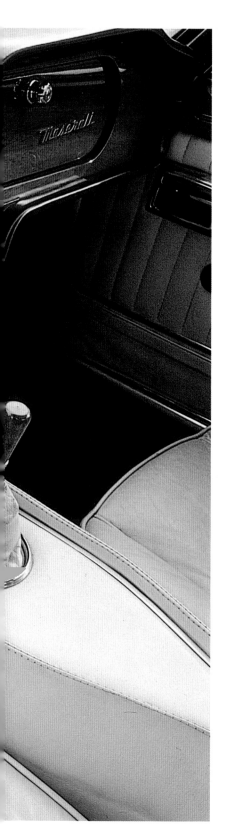

Above

A set of wire wheels gives something of a clue to the nature of the beast, which could at first glance look like a fairly ordinary coupé

Left

More leather, more rich and comfortable materials for the Mexico, as Maserati move into the luxury grand touring market

Above
The dramatic lines of the Indy presage a move to bigger and more luxurious cars, but with 260bhp, performance is not compromised

Above right
Not many cars are capable of carrying four people at a genuine top speed of 150mph in any degree of comfort

Right
The Indy was not only comfortable for four adults; its practical luggage capacity made it a genuine Grand Tourer

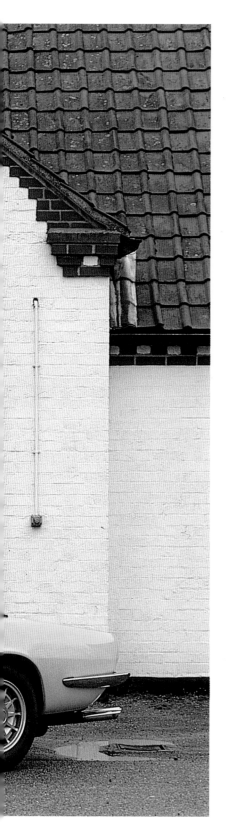

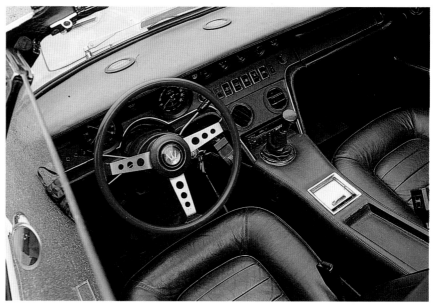

Above

Looking over the back of a Ghibli convertible, the interior and dash are obviously designed for grand touring in speed and comfort

Left

The Ghibli was a design from the pen of Ghia, a two-seater fitted with the 4.9 litre V8, giving it a top speed of nearly 170mph

Above

The fisheye lens can of course make a Morris Minor look aggressive; but the Ghibli's looks really did live up to what was under the hood

Above right

The Ghibli logo features the Maserati trident from the fountain of Neptune in Bologna, albeit in a more stylised form than usual

Right

The rare convertible version of the Ghibli featured a neat cover for the fully retractable hood, which clipped down to cover it completely

Above
Across the smooth skin of the Ghibli, there are distinct hints of the muscles it contains

Right
The retractable headlights are less than entirely elegant: but at a hundred and fifty miles per hour you want to see where you're going

Above
The high rear quarters of the Ghibli coupé enclose a luggage area that would take more Vuitton cases than most sports saloons

Left
Lovely balanced styling and as much power, handling and comfort as you can use – who could ask more of a Grand Tourer?

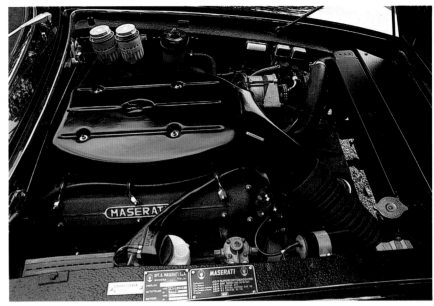

Above
Five litres and 340bhp of delicately orchestrated muscle. There's no substitute for cubes, but for Maserati that's just the starting point

Left
The office of the Maserati Ghibli. Not much evidence of the racing origins of the car here, apart from the numbers on the speedometer

The Supercars of the Seventies

Maserati's first rear mid-engined, road-going supercar was the Bora, announced in November 1971. It was named after the wind that blows around Trieste, and follows the wind theme of the Ghibli and the Mistrale. Giulio Alfieri had taken Maserati's experience on the racetrack with the Tipo 63 and 65 sports racers of the early Sixties and, of course, the Cooper-Maserati Grand Prix car. The basic design was then shipped over to Giugiaro at Ital design. Giugiaro produced a body in steel that combined muscle and delicacy, with a hunched, purposefully high rear and a curvy front end, suggesting the mid-engined configuration without making a fuss about it.

The practicality had still been retained, unusually for a mid-engined supercar, as there was a reasonably substantial luggage compartment under the bonnet at the front. An interesting idea was the storage of the battery in a drawer on the rear wall of this compartment: after all, the battery does have to be accessible, but not very often. Also clever was the provision of a luggage space for briefcases and so on inside the cabin, using the space occupied on the other side by the petrol tank. You don't generally get this sort of forethought in most mid-engined cars.

The 22 gallon fuel tank may sound excessive, but with the mileage per gallon averaging around 12, the car needed a decent sized tank to have a realistic touring range. With a magazine reporting a genuine and usable top speed of 168mph, the Bora in the hands of an enthusiastic driver would drink petrol at a prodigious rate. The press in general felt that the car's weight and relatively small 215/70 section tyres limited its performance, but they all seemed to feel it could be used every day of the year, which can't be said about most mid-engined supercars.

The interior and driveability of the Bora was well up to the mark even by Maserati's standards, with thick leather and even thicker carpeting

The Bora, with coachwork by Ital Design. The mid-engined configuration sacrificed practicality for pure performance

everywhere, and with Alfieri raiding the parts bins and ideas files of
Maserati's new owner Citroën to great effect.

The steering wheel was adjustable to pretty well exactly where you
wanted it, and the pedals went back and forward on a button, while the
seats were adjustable for rake and for height. The pop-up headlights
worked through a pumped-up reserve tank with the pressure maintained
by the engine. Less popular was the over-sensitive button braking system
from the Citroën stable, which results in an undignified four-wheel slide if
used with insufficient delicacy, although it actually stops the car very well
when you get the hang of it.

The engine for the Bora was a light alloy 90° V8 with four overhead
cams and a capacity of 4719cc. The engine produced 310bhp, and
powered the car to a maximum speed of 168mph, fairly respectable
when compared with the competition. Transmission was a 5-speed ZF

*Rather than luggage space, the rear
hatch of the Bora opened to reveal a
4,719cc quad-cam V8 of 310bhp*

The mounting of the engine/gearbox/transmission package kept noise and vibration to a minimum as well as making repairs and servicing easier

box, and carburation involved four Weber DCNFs. The entire engine and rear suspension system was incorporated in a detachable sub-frame, which bolted onto the monocoque Bora chassis. The routine servicing of the engine would be done from above, but for anything major the entire power and drivetrain package, comprising the engine, gearbox, driveshafts, suspension and wheels, could be removed within two hours.

This drive system packaging arrangement also kept vibration and noise to a minimum by isolating the whole engine and drive from the cabin, and kept the car acceptably civilised to drive: quite a tricky business to achieve, with four cams thrashing round just a few inches from the driver's ear.

The construction of the chassis also reflected imagination and foresight. It is notoriously hard work to get a rear-engined car through crash testing, because the engine acts as another 'boot up the backside',

rather than absorbing some of the impact (which it does if positioned at the front). However, the Bora went straight through the test first time.

About 500 Boras were built, both in 4.7-litre and 4.9-litre formats. Overall the car was a big success, and it certainly helped change the public view of Maserati as a company.

The Merak first appeared at the Paris show, rather than the more usual Turin launch. Essentially the car was a development of the Bora, redefined as a result of the involvement of Citroën in the company, and using a version of the engine Maserati had developed for the Citroën-Maserati SM, with the same gearbox as the one used in that model, but mounted the other way round in the car. The trademark rear pillars of the Merak followed something close to the line of the Bora's rear end, but the actual rear window was a short vertical slit.

The Merak was technically a two plus two, but we are really talking about two plus an extremely small two. The car was similar to the Bora in its blend of Citroën and Maserati, and it incorporated Citroën

Above
The trademark flying buttresses on the back of the Merak said it was a close cousin to the Bora, but also something new in its own right

Left
The Merak was the product of the Citroën/Maserati relationship, and used a smaller three litre V6 in a reworked Bora body

instruments, the high-pressure braking system and the single spoke steering wheel from the Citroën parts bins. The use of the engine designed by Maserati for the SM was quite a different strategy from the thinking behind the Bora, and was aimed at a different type of buyer: it was more for use as an upmarket businessman's express than for well-heeled performance enthusiasts.

The introduction of different sized front and rear tyres meant there was no longer much point in trying to carry a full-sized spare, so a much smaller American-style emergency spare was now fitted in the engine bay. The six-cylinder engine, being short a couple of cylinders, also left a little extra room for manoeuvre, so the cabin space could be considerably increased. Again scoring in practicality, fuel consumption while cruising at sensible cross country speeds could get up to as much as 24mpg, and at 100mph was around 20mph, which is not at all bad by anyone's standards, and for a car like this 17mpg in town driving was pretty respectable too.

Smart moves in product rationalisation could also be seen as a result of Citroën's involvement: if you bought a left-hand-drive Merak you got what was essentially an SM dash and interior. Right-hand-drive interiors were almost invariably sourced from the Bora parts bins. The carburation differed, although the basic engine was shared as well: in the

Above
The interior of the Merak still managed to be comfortable despite the mid engined configuration, which is not as easy as it sounds

Above right
One of the many problems generated by rear mounted engines is getting air out of the engine compartment: hence the multitudinous louvres

Right
The luggage capacity of the Merak was not one of its major selling points, and is limited to just a spare wheel and a packed lunch

SM you would get Bosch fuel injection, but the Maserati featured three twin-choke 42DCNF Webers. Well, with the best will in the world, you can't get the right noise out of an injection system, can you?

The redefined SM engine fitted to the Merak was a 2,965cc V6, producing 190bhp and 188 ft/lbs of torque at 4,000rpm, enough for nearly 150mph in the light and streamlined Merak. As the car developed into the Merak SS, the engine was redeveloped by Alfieri to produce more power. At the same time, the car lost 330lbs in weight, so the later models were appreciably quicker. There was also a 2-litre version developed in response to Italian tax laws relating to engine size. A total of 1,700 Meraks were built by Maserati before production ended in 1983: overall, the car was a considerable success.

In many ways the Khamsin, concurrent for some years with the rear-engined cars, was retrogressive: it still used the venerable quad-cam

The design of the Merak, while referring very strongly to the Bora, still managed to suggest that it was a cousin rather than a clone

Every line of the body is just where it should be: the Merak looks as though it is doing 100mph, even when it's standing still

Maserati V8, and it went back to the traditional front-engine, rear-drive set-up. Many still maintain that the front mid-engine, rear-drive arrangement is the best and indeed the fastest configuration for a practical, very high speed road car, and while the Khamsin only sold four hundred or so, it just kept on quietly being made as the years went by.

The development costs of the car were not outrageous in any case, as it had been developed from the basis of the De Tomaso Longchamp, taking advantage of Alejandro de Tomaso's heavy involvement with Maserati. The Khamsin was intended to satisfy the buyers who had been interested in the Indy; those who may not have been excited by the idea of mid-engined supercars, but who still wanted a straightforward Maserati Grand Tourer.

With the 4,930 cc quad cam V8 kicking out a substantial 320bhp, the Khamsin was not exactly sluggish: top speed was around 170mph, and

the 0-60 acceleration was recorded at 6.6 seconds. For a car this size, that is eminently respectable.

The Khamsin's body, by Bertone, was a very modern interpretation of the traditional sports car format, and indeed mostly consisted of bonnet, which stretched out in front of the driver like a Bugatti Type 41. The visual weight of the body was right down low, with big wide alloy wheels and a thin and understated roofline. Again showing the commitment to getting it right, irrespective of the cost, the engine was dry sumped in order to get it low enough to keep the bonnet line right down. Following the GT tradition, there was a considerable acreage of richly carpeted storage space in the back, although the two supposed rear seats were more theoretical than practical.

The seats and steering wheel were very adjustable, so pretty well anyone could find a comfortable position for long trips, and the Khamsin was notable for another of those small details that make cars special: in the passenger footwell there was a little footrest, just in the right place.

Left
The early Khamsin, which replaced the Indy as Maserati's premium Grand Tourer, and was powered by the faithful 4.9 litre V8

Above
The traditional front engined configuration once again moved the visual weight of the cabin backwards. The spoked wheel at the back is not a standard fitment

This is the sort of thing that nobody else bothers about, but it's also the kind of nice little touch that gains unswerving loyalty among enthusiasts.

Another interesting, if unusual, idea was the servo-powered steering, which automatically returned the wheel to centre when you let go of it, even when stationary. This level of power in the steering arrangements also allowed a very direct two turns lock to lock. However, at the same time, the steering can't have been over-powered, or the press would have complained. They had nothing but praise for the car, so Maserati somehow solved a problem here which is still baffling most car manufacturers. The clutch was also power-assisted, which made it a joy to use, but sometimes spoiled the sort of takeoffs that involve revving the engine to screaming point and then dumping the clutch: apparently it would slip just a little before letting all 320bhp through to the wheels.

The Khamsin took full advantage of the benefits of the traditional front-engined format in providing driver comfort. The mid-mounted engine configuration does have limitations in that humans have legs that

Above
The panel at the rear was made of glass: very stylish, as well as being very useful when reversing in town. Maserati brightwork is not cheap

Right
The front-engined Grand Tourer format allowed a cabin with loads of room, which was up to the mark in luxurious leather and deep carpets

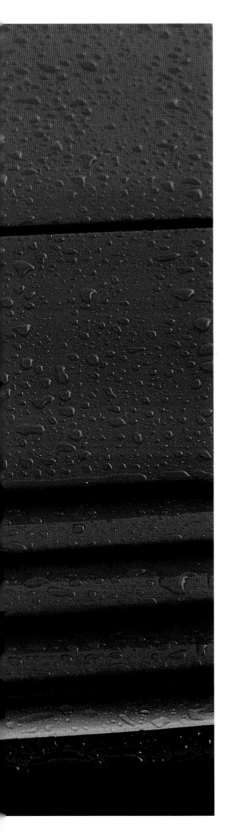

stick out in front, and with the engine where the seats should be, you have to make compromises with fitting humans into the space. In a single-seater racing car, it's no problem because your legs go between the wheels: with a mid-engine taking up the back and fat wheels and arches taking up the front, there's no good place to put feet. The Khamsin allows not only big seats with lots of adjustment and loads of elbow room, but also gives you plenty of clutch foot room and a huge luggage area at the back. In terms of pure numbers the Khamsin may only have only reached 400, but I would be prepared to bet that the 400 customers were very happy with them.

The 1976 Kyalami was one of Alejandro de Tomaso's ideas. Essentially it was a De Tomaso Longchamp, with minor bodywork alterations by Frua. The Longchamp's cooking-quality Ford Cleveland 5,763cc single cam V8 with a single Motorcraft carb was removed, along with its Cruise-o-Matic automatic transmission. Not quite the thing, really.

The Ford engine was replaced with the familiar Maserati 4,930cc V8,

Above
The Khamsin's big wheels and high waist went a lot of the way to suggesting the serious performance of the car, which went as fast as it looked

Left
During the Seventies, the three-pronged trident graced the bonnets of some of the most beautiful and potent cars in the world

Above left

The big V8 sat well back in the Khamsin chassis, with most of the weight under the windscreen: the weight distribution would be just about perfect

Left

Although much attention is paid to the comfort and luxury touches in Maserati's interiors, the ergonomics are clearly pretty good as well

Above

The big haunches and dropped nose of the Khamsin serve to accentuate its purpose, which is very high speed travel in luxurious comfort

and the car was re-christened the Kyalami after the racing circuit. However, after 190 sales, the Kyalami version of the car quietly faded from sight, leaving the De Tomaso Longchamp to carry on in GTS and cabriolet forms.

The Quattroporte concept came back around in 1974 with the introduction of a Bertone-bodied five-seater saloon car available originally with a V6, of which only five were made, and later graduating to the V8, of which a couple of thousand were made. The idea was to provide serious luxury and high performance, with acres of padded leather and deeply veneered wood.

The styling was sensible to the point of being anodyne, and the car had no instant Maserati look about it: the approach to the Quattroporte was more a matter of taking the BMW 7-series and adding flavour and style to it, particularly with the delicious sound of a Maserati V8 being given some stick. At that point the message would get across that this was not part of the ordinary run of European autobahn cruisers.

Above
*The Kyalami, named after the South African Grand Prix circuit, was in fact a reworked
De Tomaso Longchamp, with a restyle by Frua*

Right
*Beneath the bonnet of the De Tomaso's Kyalami lurked a pure Maserati V8, providing
true Maserati performance: 280bhp and 150mph*

The Biturbo Generation

The first Biturbo was introduced in 1982. It was a complete departure from the quad-cam V8 powered supercars, and very much of its time. From the flowing lines and big engines of the Seventies, the Biturbo was a subtle collection of sharp edges and high technology: its performance was hidden under a body that at first glance could have been a production Ford. Well, perhaps not a Ford, but possibly an Audi.

The confidence that lay behind the understatement of the general look of the car could perhaps be explained to some extent by the badge in the centre of the steering wheel – it was the same badge that had graced the nose of the first Maserati racing cars of 1926. The driver got the Tipo 26 badge to remind him where he was, and the public got to see the trident on the front of the grille where they might have expected to see the four rings of Audi or the propeller of BMW.

The new Biturbo V6 engine was only two litres in size, but its twin turbochargers boosted the power up to 180bhp. The car could be sold for sensible money, although it would never be cheap, and the sales figures for the Biturbo in 1983 rose to 6,000, thus giving Maserati their best sales year ever.

Rather than a new big Quattroporte, the next model to be introduced was the 425 Biturbo of 1983, with the engine enlarged to 2500cc and the bodywork re-thought to provide four seats without compromising the line or balance of the car. Top speed was 130mph, respectable enough for a family sized car, and sales for the year again topped the 6,000 mark.

Lee Iacocca, who coincidentally had been responsible for putting the Ford engine in the De Tomaso cars, now got Chrysler involved with Maserati with a view to making a Chrysler-Maserati sports car, powered by a Lotus engine. This, however, failed to materialise in any serious sense. Maserati had certainly been very helpful in supplying engines for all sorts of specials for several generations – Ligier-Maserati, Talbot-Maserati. Lister-Maserati, Cooper-Maserati. It is not immediately clear why one

A complete departure from exclusive quad-cam five litre supercars, the Biturbo was a blend of high technology and design understatement

112

Above left

Just in case the body design was too subtle, there is the occasional reminder that this is not a run-of-the-mill coupé

Left

The anachronistic but rather attractive oval clock is another Maserati trademark. (Can a clock be anachronistic? Don't even think about it.)

Above

A Maserati graces the banking at Brooklands. It would be a pleasure to see Maserati back in racing, although it seems unlikely

would go in with Maserati on a project that used a Lotus engine, but I imagine they had their reasons.

For 1984, the top came off the Biturbo to offer a Spyder version of the car, and each year saw new developments of the same theme. 1985 saw the 420S with fuel injection and four doors, although it was just a quattro porte rather than a Quattroporte. In 1987, the enlarged 2.8-litre version of the engine was introduced in the 430, which saw the performance beginning to creep back up to the sort of levels that had traditionally been associated with the name Maserati.

The Karif was a pretty and purposeful looking coupé version of the same squared off, clean body style. The Karif was as understated as the first of the Biturbos had been when they were first announced in 1982. 1989 also saw the introduction of the 222, featuring two doors, two litres and two cams. The later 224 featured 24 valves and two turbos.

Fiat bought 49% of Maserati in 1989, which allowed sufficient capitalisation to let Maserati get back into what they did best, which has always involved seriously high performance and relatively low volumes of production. Nonetheless, the whole Biturbo story reflects rather well on the company in that they successfully changed direction and fought well against considerable competition.

The emergence of the Shamal took Maserati right back up to the top

Above left
Unashamed luxury. A vast acreage of leather and exotic woods, and the trademark chronometer to remind you what you're driving

Left
Mismatched veneers in the Maserati interior are odd: however, the wheel and gear knob match, so the different coloured cappings must be deliberate

Above
The convertible version of the Biturbo loses nothing in the translation from the coupe: both are unmistakably subtle, understated and stylish

of the league of practical supercars. Just because it goes extremely quickly is no reason not to provide four seats and a boot. The body of the Shamal is recognisably a direct descendant of the earlier Biturbos, but it's as if the Biturbo was bitten by a rabid dog somewhere along the way! The look of the car is aggressive, hunched and poised.

The Maserati signature cut-out of the rear wheel arches seen in the birdcage racers of thirty years ago came back to add yet more understated menace to the presence of the Shamal, and some more purposeful elements also contributed to the design. The central roof pillar, painted black and badged with a Shamal logo, covers up a substantial roll over bar. The bar across the front of the windscreen, continuing the line of the front roof pillars, certainly looks sleek. It also keeps the screen clean at very high speeds, and keeps the wipers on the glass.

The heart of the Shamal has to be its engine. Maserati couldn't resist the delicious howl of a quad-cam V8, and went back to that format for the Shamal. The engine is 3217cc, with four valves per cylinder. The by now familiar twin water-cooled turbos and Weber-Marelli fuel injection cram in even more mixture than the last generation of Maseratis, which used to suck in through massed ranks of twin-choke Webers.

The engine is certainly not a leftover from the past in terms of its design, although the basic format is historic Maserati. It is light alloy with

Left

Most of the offset of this relatively wide wheel is concealed inside the wheel arch: no need for any ostentatiously wide rims

Above

The Shamal catapulted Maserati straight back into the supercar arena: 430bhp on tap, handling to match, and still a practical car

the Vee angle at 90°, and the bore and stroke at 80 x 80, which is conventional, but the treatment of the management system is bang up to date. Each bank of cylinders is managed as a separate system, with an interface between the two control units. Total failure is thus unlikely, and the car remains driveable. This same philosophy also applies to the twin fuel pumps.

With the engine completed, the transmission was next. Getrag provided a six-speed gearbox which was capable of handling the powerful 436Nm of torque put out by the engine without disintegrating into an ally box full of swarf. The box also had to change swiftly and easily without giving a clue as to its agricultural strength.

At the back, Maserati had already developed their own torque-sensing differential, which was fitted to the Shamal. This set-up could apply 92% of the engine's power to whichever wheel had the most grip. The Maserati system is also notably smooth in doing this, which is absolutely crucial in high speed driving. If you're pushing your luck anywhere near the limit, the last thing you want is an unexpected jerk of extra power.

The 'old-fashioned' format of front engine, gearbox in the middle and driving axle at the back is only old fashioned in the sense that vintage wine is old-fashioned. It is worth knowing, perhaps, that TVR's Peter Wheeler also builds his cars that way in the UK. He could build them any way he wants, and his design team continually urge him to let them play with mid engines. But he declines. The fastest cross country car on real roads is rear wheel drive with the front wheels free, so that's the way they build them. I know myself that I drive mid-engined cars much more slowly because I don't like the feel of being between the engine and whatever I hit should something go seriously wrong.

So we don't see Maserati shying away from either old or new ideas: they just pick and choose the best from what's on offer. Electronics are extensively used in the suspension on the Shamal, which was developed by Koni in Germany. Intelligent damping means that each wheel's activity is reported back to a central computer which affects the other wheels in relation to the signal from the first. The whole thing is also controllable by the driver, with four levels of ride firmness available at the mere touch of a switch.

There's no ABS on the brakes. This seems an odd thing to leave out, with all the other electronics that have been fitted to the car, so it must have been left out by choice. Perhaps it's Maserati's view that braking is best left to the judgement and skill of the driver, perhaps it's that the Shamal is only really intended for people who want to drive by the soles of their feet and their fingers on the wheel. Lots of grip at the back is a good idea, instantly adjustable suspension is a good idea, but perhaps the retention of control in a precarious situation by the controlled application of pulsed braking is something we want to keep control of, rather than handing over that particular decision to a box of electronics.

The Shamal represents Maserati's return to the top rank of supercar manufacturers. Compared with some, it is understated, subtle, and won't do over 200mph in a straight line. However, I would not be at all surprised to find that across country on genuine everyday roads it is one of the fastest cars in the world. Even if this is not the case, it deserves a place in the very top ranks just for the pure bliss of listening to the utterly delicious chords of a quad cam V8 with two turbos howling away under full power!

The glossy, rake-adjustable, fat wooden steering wheel feels slightly dead in a straight line, but comes alive at every corner

The Maserati Experience

I decided it was time to go and play with a Maserati. It was a tough job, but someone had to do it. I called Meridien Maserati down in Lyndhurst in Hampshire, and asked if they would allow me to take a Ghibli out, with a view to discovering what it can do.

A Shamal would have been the more obvious choice, but I was more interested in a Maserati that the ordinary motorist might just possibly be able to afford one day. The Shamal costs £55,000 as we go to press, and will graduate from very expensive new car to cherished classic without even noticing the change. The Ghibli, on the other hand, costs about £43,000. There will be more Ghiblis made than Shamals, and there is a possibility that their value may come down and be within the reach of a wider market. An old Biturbo, for example, can be bought for a sensible amount of money nowadays. The Shamal may remain a dream, but a Ghibli, just maybe, one day. . .

"You want a Ghibli to play with? No problem," said Meridien, being helpful and accommodating sort of people. "Just pop down when it suits you and we'll sort something out."

I drove down to Lyndhurst in an old Triumph special I've had for years, partly to provide myself with the maximum contrast with the Maserati. The old Triumph has a 2-litre six in it, only weighs half-a-ton or so and goes quite quickly, but after a recent conversion to a live rear axle from the horrible Triumph independent rear end, the suspension is as yet unsorted and the ride is as supple as a trolley jack.

Also, the silencer, such as it is, has suffered an internal haemorrhage. So the exhaust note is fruity under acceleration, which is quite fun, but on a long run it does drone on. The heater blower is broken, too, and the hood doesn't fit. When I arrived exhausted, fairly cold and with my ears ringing slightly, even a Ford Fiesta would have looked quite good. How would a Maserati look by comparison with the Midge? Rather incredible, I should say.

The Ghibli in question sat there looking pretty pleased with itself, as well it might. It was a year or so old, and had done 9000 miles or so. Nicely run in and raring to go. It was silver with a cream coloured

Above right
A 1993 Ghibli continues the Biturbo line: although extremely fast, it is still very understated in design, although more ostentatious inside

Right
The Ghibli looks more aggressive from this angle, which is – to make a well-worn auto journalist's point – the angle from which most people will see the car as it hurtles past them

leather interior, and at first glance looked good, but nothing special: quite a lot like an Audi Quattro or Coupé in fact, particularly as it was silver. It was fun watching people glance at it parked in the garage by the Meridien showroom, then seeing them do a double take when they realised it was something special rather than just another sports saloon.

Subtlety is a big part of the nature of most current Maseratis. While a red Ferrari screams 'look at me, look at me, I'm extremely fast and very, very expensive,' and everyone cranes their neck to peer inside in the hope of seeing a footballer or a pop star, the Maserati is quite content to pass relatively unnoticed except by the cognoscenti. While taking the pictures of the car in the New Forest, I parked it in the middle of a dirt road. Someone in a rather nice old Rover 100 came by. The first expression on his face was irritation at someone blocking the road, followed by fascination and delight when he realised it was a Maserati. At that point I realised that even though it doesn't even have a badge on the front saying Maserati or Ghibli, just a small chrome trident is sufficient – no need for any fuss.

There is, however, a fair bit to make a fuss about. 5.7 seconds to 60 mph and a top speed of around 160mph is more than respectable, although more important is the grunt when you want to overtake something and get back on to your own side of the road before anything untoward happens: no shortage of that either in the Ghibli, as it happens. The engine is a development of the early Biturbo idea, enlarged from the original two litres to 2790cc to bring in a fair bit of torque as well as the howl: 311 lb/ft, to be exact. So if you wanted to cruise around in the lower reaches of the rev counter without waking the turbos up, you could still make reasonable progress.

The engine is pure Maserati, an all-alloy 280bhp V6 with four cams driving four valves per cylinder. As we go to press, a new direct ignition system is taking the place of ignition coils. The fuel system has been electronic for some time, and the twin turbos have been a familiar Maserati feature for a decade now.

The gearbox is a five-speed, and the rear axle is the sophisticated Maserati limited-slip affair known as the Ranger. A tiny detail that speaks volumes is that the rear axle has an oil cooler. This would rather suggest that the rear axle is expected to do some warm work.

Anyway, that's enough of the theory. What is the Maserati Ghibli actually like?

Walk across the forecourt to where the car sits, looking squat and purposeful. The big silver door swings open, and you slide into the cool, slick leather seat. Pull the door shut, which takes a bit of doing – it's a solid, heavy affair and it closes with a meaty thud.

The driving position is utterly Italian, rather cramped on legroom and

The 3 litre twin-turbocharged V6 of the Ghibli: tame town driving, or an exhilarating kick in the back if you leave your foot down

the steering wheel is quite far from the body. I am more used to a vintage driving position, with a huge steering wheel a few inches away from my chest. The rather lovely thick wooden steering wheel on the Ghibli was thus some distance away from the ideal spot. However, I found the seat back button and silently upped the seat back, then looked for the seat forwards button. What seat forwards button? After a bit of searching I had a grope under the seat and, sure enough, there was a metal bar. This I found endearingly daft. If you're going for electric seats, why on earth stop halfway?

If you're going to do any serious driving it is quite important to have everything where you expect it – I found myself fumbling around for pedals once on an utterly irreplaceable 1936 Jaguar SS100 as I charged towards an unexpectedly sharp corner with large and substantial trees blocking any possible escape route, and it was not one of my favourite experiences. Fortunately, pre-war Jags handle better than I had any right to expect, and I had time to get disentangled and back on to the throttle

So where is everything on the Ghibli? Instruments all sensibly placed, all visible. Pedals closer together and further over to the left than you would expect, but no problem once you know where they are. Clutch firm, quite a big throttle pedal. Left side of the steering column for the indicators, and they're a bit tacky. Mind you, the major controls are actually very impressive. The wheel is silky smooth, leather faced, and varnished deep enough to go for a paddle in it. The gear lever and handbrake are in the same gorgeous wood and – get this – the gear lever has the R,1,2,3,4,5 engraved into its top. A lovely little touch, that.

Now for the moment of truth. Turn the key and the starter panics and sets up a fast, turbine chittering until there's a crack and a chumble from under the bonnet, and the V6 bursts into life, revving and settling as the electronics wake up. A Christmas tree of warning lights disappears in a sequence as the Ghibli sorts itself out. Chunk into first, and delicately amble out on to the road, then tiptoe through Lyndhurst without any embarrassing tyre squealing, until I can find a bit of clear road. Right turn. Tinka, tinka, clear, off we go. An injudicious poke on the throttle, and there's a definite twitch from the back as the tyres scrabble for grip.

Take it easy until the turbos have warmed up, and have a look around the interior. The deep wood of the wheel, handbrake and gear lever is a completely different colour from the light maple colour of the slugs of wood on the dash and the doors. Why? Who knows, but they must have done it on purpose. The leather on the doors is very grainy and very obviously leather. The dash top is grey suede, presumably to avoid distracting reflections: it works. Even the grab handles for getting out of the back seat are covered in hand-stitched cream leather, and everyone in the car gets their own little reading light let into the roof.

The steering feels oddly dead in the straight ahead position, and livens up a little when you switch to a different suspension setting. There are four of these, ranging from the physically comfortable firmish default setting that the car chooses when you switch it on, to a mentally comfortable, rather more firmish setting which reassures you that you won't get any unexpected body roll to put you off your line in a fast corner. With a corner in progress and the steering wheel turned, it comes alive in your hands and you can feel exactly what's going on.

A nice straight beckons, and I put my foot right down in second. There's a growl and an increase in speed from the torque of the engine. Then the turbos join in, and with a definite whistle they give the Ghibli a huge bootful of power that rams it forwards. Six thousand, third, back on the throttle hard, more whistles, more kick in the back; this thing is seriously fast, and seriously competent. Brake, no fuss, steady and

The new Quattroporte demonstrates that the family man or woman can have their focaccia and eat it. Maserati's four-door saloon is more exciting than most manufacturers' sports cars

poised, next corner, half throttle and let the power come in as the turbos spin up, loads of grip, solid and sure, out the other end and now let rip.

There isn't a turbo lag as such – what you really have is a two-step throttle. There's a gap between not going fast and going fast, but once you're up there with the turbos whistling, power is instant, whenever you want it, until you let the revs die down to cruising levels. In some ways it feels like the two-step throttle on a Carter mechanical carb I had on a 5.7-litre Cobra replica once, in which half the throttle movement worked two reasonable sized barrels or chokes. If you went beyond the step, two extra monster barrels opened up, a thump of power slammed in and you had to be ready to catch the rear end. However, that sort of power was just low down grunt from sheer size, not the beautifully orchestrated cacophony of cams and valves that gives the blend of mid and high range punch from the Maserati engine. The Chevy engine shook your spine, the Maserati shakes your preconceptions.

Sharp corner, 100 metres ahead, brake medium hard, scrub off the speed nice and smooth, dab the throttle and down into third, dab second, slow down hard, on to the apex and open up to come rocketing out of it, but this time there's a protest from the back and a decided twitch. The Ghibli's handling is excellent, and way beyond the capabilities of anything else that looks like a four-seater coupé, but it has its limits. Nevertheless, you feel exactly what's going on, with plenty of warning.

There are a few rear-engined and mid-engined exotica that can certainly outdo the Ghibli in terms of sheer G-force on a corner, but they won't necessarily warn you when you're pushing your luck: they'll just wait for the right moment and then try to kill you. I think this may be a reflection on the way the cars are developed: all the major manufacturers have proper test tracks where they can tune suspension and geometry to precise levels. All Maserati have is the roads around the factory, some of which are pretty demanding. Maserati's cars inevitably become very good at going as fast as is practical across country on real roads. Which is, after all, what we want them to be able to do.

ABS braking will be available on Ghiblis from now on, but it will only be there as an option. I wouldn't want it myself. The brakes are very sensitive and progressive, and you can feel exactly what's going on – I'd rather retain the feedback and control of them through my feet. After all, the driver is supposed to be driving in a car like this.

Stop for some snaps, and another endearing idiosyncrasy arises: the turbo gauge records a big boost when the radiator cooling fans switch on. I haven't a clue as to why that should happen. Nor do I care; I just like that sort of thing. It happens on handbuilt cars like Maseratis, and doesn't happen on Ford Escorts.

The boot on the Ghibli takes my camera case and tripods with acres of room left over: it's actually the same size as in most family saloon cars. The back seats are occasional items rather than serious passenger seats, but you could genuinely use a Maserati Ghibli as an everyday car.

It's very much two completely different cars in one. For the Jekyll persona, stay off the loud pedal, take it easy and you've got nicely luxurious long distance transport. To transform the Ghibli into the Hyde character, just leave your foot on the throttle for an extra second until you hear the whistle of the turbos.

The current Maserati line-up of Ghibli, Shamal and the new Quattroporte are different from the earlier Maseratis, but they are still well within the tradition of the company: all pretty, all extremely fast, and all conceived and designed for drivers who get the same thrill that Maserati do out of fast, beautiful cars.

If Fiat understand this and take steps to protect it, Maserati can continue to produce designs with power, style and character. We will have to hope that they deal with Maserati using the lightest of touches.